COAST 2 COAST 2 COAST

WELCOME TO NEW FRANCE

ROAD TO
UPPER AND
LOWER CANADA

BY JANET SLINGERLAND

Coast2Coast2Coast is published by Beech Street Books
27 Stewart Rd. Collingwood, ON Canada L9Y 4M7

www.beechstreetbooks.ca

Produced by Red Line Editorial

Photographs ©: North Wind Picture Archives, cover, 1, 14–15, 17, 25; Felix Lipov/Shutterstock Images, 4–5; Red Line Editorial, 6, 11, 29; V.J. Matthew/Shutterstock Images, 8–9; Charles William Jefferys/Library and Archives Canada/Acc. No. 1972-26-768, 13; William Pether/Library of Congress, 18–19; Franz Xaver Habermann/Library of Congress, 20; Henry Alexander Ogden/Library of Congress, 22–23; Warren Price Photography/Shutterstock Images, 26–27

Editor: Amanda Lanser
Designer: Nikki Farinella

Library and Archives Canada Cataloguing in Publication

Slingerland, Janet, author
       Road to Upper and Lower Canada / by Janet Slingerland.

(Welcome to New France)
Includes bibliographical references and index.
Issued in print and electronic formats.
ISBN 978-1-77308-020-8 (hardback).--ISBN 978-1-77308-048-2 (paperback).--
ISBN 978-1-77308-076-5 (pdf).--ISBN 978-1-77308-104-5 (html)

       1. Canada--History--1713-1763 (New France)--Juvenile literature.
2. Canada--History--1763-1791--Juvenile literature. I. Title.

 FC305.S64 2016   j971.01'8   C2016-903637-5
                                                    C2016-903638-3

Printed in the United States of America
Mankato, MN
August 2016

TABLE OF CONTENTS

CLASS SYSTEM IN NEW FRANCE

In 1750 France's colony in North America, New France, was home to 55,000 colonists. They spoke French and practised the Catholic religion. Many lived in Quebec and Montreal, the colony's two largest cities. The cities were in the northeast region of the colony. Most of New France's territory was still **frontier**.

Seigneurs, Habitants, and Traders

New France operated under a **feudal** system. The king granted land to wealthy colonists along the St. Lawrence River. The land owners were called *seigneurs*. The colony's first seigneurs were nobles and religious orders.

Notre Dame des Victoires in Quebec City was completed in 1723.

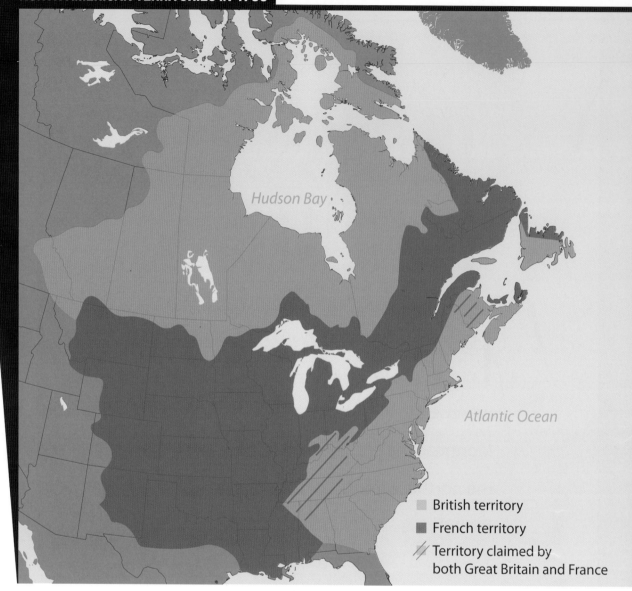

Hudson Bay

Atlantic Ocean

British territory
French territory
Territory claimed by both Great Britain and France

Seigneurs rented out their land to poorer colonists called habitants. The habitants worked the land. They grew crops and raised livestock. They had to produce enough to pay taxes and rent to their seigneur.

Traders and merchants made up New France's middle class. They imported European goods. They exported furs from the colony to France. Some traded goods with First Nations communities. Many **Aboriginal** Peoples trapped animals for fur to trade with the colonists.

Unfriendly Neighbours

France competed with Great Britain for North American territory. More than 1 million British colonists lived in 13 colonies along the Atlantic Coast. This population was growing rapidly. Small conflicts broke out between France and Great Britain over land and resources.

CLASS SYSTEM IN NEW FRANCE

Seigneurs – Habitants – Traders

CHAPTER TWO

FRENCH AND BRITISH TENSIONS BUILD

France and Great Britain both had claims to territory in North America. The continent was just one place over which France and Great Britain fought. The countries had long-standing conflicts in Europe and elsewhere in the world. Both wanted to lay claim to the resources in North America, including those in New France. Great Britain wanted to extend its territory north, while France wanted to do the same south.

A reconstruction of a trading post from the 1600s in Nova Scotia, an area where both the French and British had claims

In the 1500s and 1600s, the countries fought over land claims. French and British explorers were nearly always armed. The military defended and managed forts and settlements. France and Great Britain led attacks on each other's forts and settlements. Both sides enlisted the support of Aboriginal Peoples. The Algonquin, Innu, and Huron-Wendat **allied** with the French. The Iroquois **Confederacy** sided with the British. France and Great Britain also fought in the wars between their Aboriginal allies. By the 1750s these tensions reached a breaking point.

Trouble in Acadia

The region of Acadia was one of the first European settlements in North America. In the early 1600s, French colonists settled among the First Nations. This land was originally the home of the Mi'kmaq, Malicite, and Abenaki communities. It included New Brunswick, Nova Scotia, and Prince Edward Island. It also included portions of Quebec.

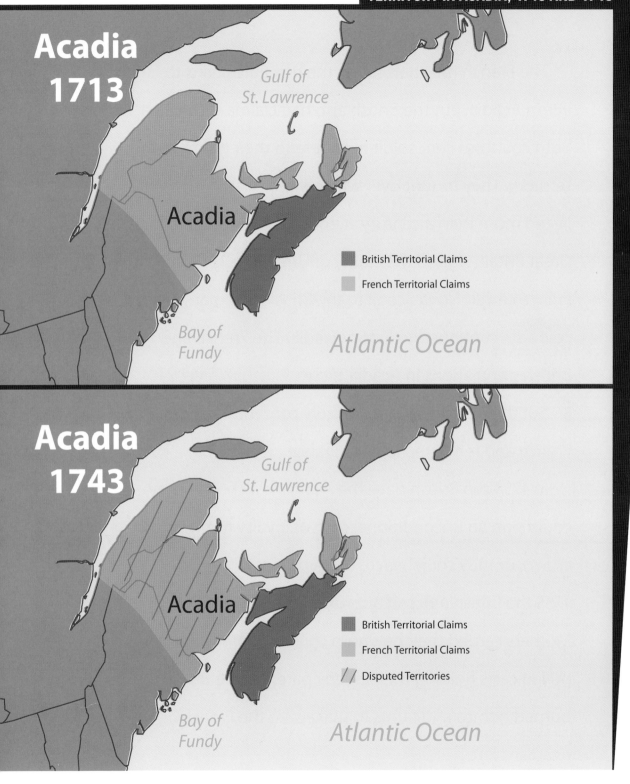

Acadia 1713

Gulf of St. Lawrence

Acadia

British Territorial Claims

French Territorial Claims

Bay of Fundy

Atlantic Ocean

Acadia 1743

Gulf of St. Lawrence

Acadia

British Territorial Claims

French Territorial Claims

Disputed Territories

Bay of Fundy

Atlantic Ocean

The French may have been the first Europeans to live in Acadia. But the British also had claims in the area. Both countries sent soldiers to defend their claims in the territory. They fought over who owned Acadia. The feud lasted more than a century. It ended when France and Great Britain signed the Treaty of Utrecht in 1713. In it France **ceded** Nova Scotia to the British. But many French colonists continued to live in Acadia. The French and British populations in Acadia grew.

But the Acadians were not truly content. They were French and remained loyal to France.

In 1754 the British gave the Acadians a choice. They could sign an unconditional oath of loyalty to the British crown, or they could leave. The Acadians refused. In 1755 the British **evicted** approximately 10,000 Acadians. Mothers carried their newborn children. Family members pulled carts holding their elderly parents. The British burned homes and farms to make sure the French Acadians left.

French Acadians received their eviction order in 1755.

The fight over Acadia was one conflict in a long-standing feud between France and Great Britain. The eviction of the French Acadians was a blow to France's claims in North America. But Acadia was on the outskirts of France's territory. Montreal, Quebec, and French territory along the St. Lawrence River were better defended. French forces were able to fend off British attacks through the first half of the 1700s. But in 1759 the British led an offensive against Quebec that the French could not defend against.

CHAPTER THREE

THE SEVEN YEARS' WAR

By the 1750s tensions between France and Great Britain had reached a tipping point. Conflict had **escalated** over North American territory. By 1755 both countries had declared war on each other. The Seven Years' War had begun.

At the start of the war, the British colonies had 20 times more people than New France had. They could recruit a greater number of soldiers. The French relied on the support of their First Nations allies. The Lorette Huron-Wendat, the Abenakis, and the Montagnais fought with the French. The Iroquois fought with the British.

First Nations fought alongside French and British troops in the Seven Years' War.

Early French Victories

First Nations communities contributed significant knowledge of the land. They used **ambush** fighting tactics never before seen by the British. The French and their allies quickly got the upper hand. They won a series of impressive victories in the first few years of the war.

But with many colonists away fighting, life in New France suffered. Trade all but stopped. Farmers were away fighting and did not tend their crops. Food became scarce. The tide turned in 1758 with a string of British victories.

A WAR BY MANY NAMES

The war between France and Great Britain is known by many names. In Canada it is called the Seven Years' War. In Quebec it is the War of the Conquest. In the United States it is called the French and Indian War.

Siege in Quebec City

Quebec City was the centre of **maritime** trade in New France. The St. Lawrence River narrowed as it passed by Quebec City. A steep cliff along the banks made the

The British landed at the Plains of Abraham in Quebec City.

city a natural fortress. In 1759 British general James Wolfe decided to take Quebec City or destroy it.

That summer, the British laid **siege** to Quebec City. They lobbed thousands of cannonballs and bombs at the city. But the city did not fall. The British needed to end the siege before winter set in.

The Battle of the Plains of Abraham

On September 13, Wolfe and 4,500 troops arrived at the Plains of Abraham. This flat area lay along the St. Lawrence River in Quebec. French and Aboriginal forces were no match for career British soldiers. The Battle of the Plains of Abraham was over in 30 minutes. The British claimed victory at Quebec City. A year later, Montreal also fell to the British.

CHAPTER FOUR

BRITISH QUEBEC

The Treaty of Paris officially ended the Seven Years' War in 1763. France ceded the bulk of New France to Great Britain. It kept two small islands off the coast of modern-day Newfoundland. Now the British had to maintain peace in North America.

A Royal Proclamation

In October 1763, King George III of Great Britain issued a Royal **Proclamation**. This document acknowledged New France was now part of Great Britain. It also included new rules for colonial relationships with First Nations communities. The proclamation stated the First Nations were under British protection. It gave First Nations communities rights to the land west of New France.

British King George III won New France in 1763.

After the Quebec Act passed, there was uneasy peace in the British colonies.

The proclamation intended to ease tension between First Nations peoples and encroaching colonists. The proclamation helped maintain Great Britain's relationship with the Iroquois. It also helped Great Britain form new alliances with France's former allies.

The proclamation created a new government. It identified a governor as the leader for the territory. It called for a general assembly that would make new laws. But no assembly was ever formed. With no assembly to make laws, people did not know what the laws were. Should people still follow the French Civil Law that had governed New France? Or should they follow the British Common Law of the British colonies?

The Quebec Act

The Quebec Act of 1774 attempted to settle these issues. It gave Roman Catholics the right to hold governing roles. British Common Law ruled criminal cases. French Civil Law applied to property and civil rights cases. The Quebec Act appeased the French. But it angered British colonists.

FRAMING QUESTIONS

What effect did the settlement of British Loyalists have on the distribution of the French and English populations? What evidence can you see of this in modern Canada?

CHAPTER FIVE

ARRIVAL OF THE LOYALISTS

The Quebec Act affected not only the government of Quebec. It also redrew the North American map. It designated the Ohio Territory as part of the now-British colony of Quebec. This was the same land over which the Seven Years' War started. This angered many people in Great Britain's 13 colonies along the eastern seaboard. The colonists considered this land part of their territory. The 13 colonies were already angry with the British crown. They did not believe the king was acting in their interests. In 1775 the American colonists started a revolution.

The American Revolution started in 1775, but not all colonists supported the Patriots, shown here in their blue uniforms.

Patriot or Loyalist?

Not all colonists had a poor opinion of the crown. An estimated 20 percent of the colonists remained loyal to King George III. Some of these Loyalists actively fought against the rebel Patriots. Others simply tried to go about their lives. But the Patriots did not make that easy.

The Patriots saw Loyalists as traitors. Patriots stripped Loyalists of their rights to vote or sell land. Loyalists could not work as doctors, lawyers, or schoolteachers. Some Patriots took Loyalist homes and possessions.

A LOOK AT LOYALISTS

Loyalists came from all walks of life. Some were rich. Some were poor. Loyalists were clergymen, craftsmen, businessmen, farmers, and soldiers. Some had strong family or business ties to Great Britain. Many feared the unknown future of Patriot independence.

Fleeing North

In 1775 more than 50,000 Loyalists began fleeing the 13 colonies. More than half made their way to Quebec and Nova Scotia. The largest group relocated in 1783.

Thousands of loyalists from the 13 colonies migrated to Nova Scotia.

Many left most of their possessions behind. They faced a brand new start, often on unworked land.

The British government rewarded the dedication of these Loyalists. Each child of a Loyalist was granted 200 acres of land. The government awarded Loyalist families a mark of honour, too. The letters "U. E." follow the names of Loyalists, their children, and their descendants. The letters stand for "Unity of the Empire." The acronym is a reminder of their loyalty to Great Britain.

CHAPTER SIX

THE CREATION OF UPPER AND LOWER CANADA

Few Loyalists who moved north went to populated areas. They were reluctant to move into French-speaking regions. Approximately 30,000 Loyalists settled in Nova Scotia. Many made their homes on land the Acadians had left behind. Loyalists who moved into Quebec remained separate from the French-speaking people there.

British Loyalists settled north of the Bay of Fundy.

The Constitutional Act

Most Loyalists did not want to live under the Quebec Act. They wanted to maintain their English language and Protestant religion. Seigneurs still controlled the land in Quebec. Loyalists wanted to own their own land.

WHAT'S IN A NAME?

Upper and Lower Canada got their names from their locations on the St. Lawrence River. Upper Canada was actually southwest of Lower Canada. But one had to paddle upriver against the current to get to Upper Canada. One moved downriver with the current to Lower Canada.

Great Britain's solution was the Constitutional Act of 1791. The law split Quebec into two provinces. Upper Canada contained mainly English-speaking colonists. Lower Canada was primarily French.

Upper Canada had a freehold land system. It followed British Common Law. Lower Canada continued using the seigneurial system and French Civil Law. The act allowed for religious freedom in the colony. It did not

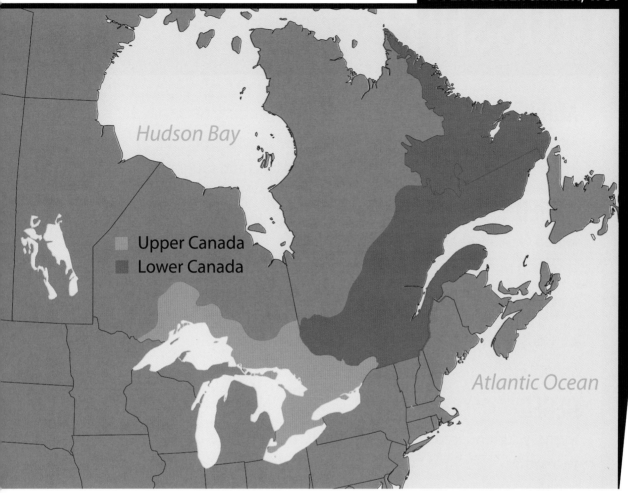

Hudson Bay

Upper Canada
Lower Canada

Atlantic Ocean

create an official language. Each province had governors who answered to the British government and an elected assembly.

The Constitutional Act allowed each province to maintain its own cultural identity. The creation of Upper and Lower Canada was the first step toward a united country culture. This united Canada still exists today.

GLOSSARY

ABORIGINAL

relating to the original inhabitants of an area

ALLIED

joined with another nation for a common purpose

AMBUSH

a surprise attack from a hidden position

CEDED

formally surrendered or gave to another

CONFEDERACY

an association of nations

ESCALATED

increased in seriousness

EVICTED

legally removed a person or persons from a property

FEUDAL

a system in which people worked land and fought for a wealthy landowner in return for protection

FRONTIER

the edge of a settled part of a country's territory

MARITIME

relating to the sea

PROCLAMATION

a formal announcement

SIEGE

a situation in which one group surrounds and isolates a city or fortress to force a surrender

TO LEARN MORE

BOOKS

Mitchell, Sara. *The Acadians*. Calgary: Weigl, 2014.

Mitchell, Sara. *The United Empire Loyalists*. Calgary: Weigl, 2014.

Wiseman, Blaine. *Battle of the Plains of Abraham*. Calgary: Weigl, 2014.

WEBSITES

Confederation for Kids
Library and Archives Canada
http://www.collectionscanada.gc.ca/confederation/kids/index-e.html

New France Around 1745
Societies and Territories
http://blogdev.learnquebec.ca/societies/societies/new-france-around-1745

Tracing the History of New France
National Archives of Canada
http://epe.lac-bac.gc.ca/100/206/301/lac-bac/new_france-ef/0517_e.html

INDEX

ABOUT THE AUTHOR

Janet Slingerland is a writer, a scout leader, and an engineer. She has a husband and three kids.